MW00955618

Crinkle

Cookie Recipes

Introduction

Crinkle cookies, which are sometimes called crackle cookies, are round cookies with cracks that are sprinkled or rolled in powder sugar so that the interior color of the cookie shows through and contrasts against the white exterior.

These cakey cookies are chewy on the inside and crispy on the outside. They are famous for the powdered sugar that creates their cracked appearance.

The original cookies were Chocolate Crinkle Cookies. These were invented by Helen Fredell in St. Paul, Minnesota in the early half of the 20th Century.

Today, variations of the traditional chocolate crinkle cookie recipe include vanilla, lemon, fudge and mint.

This cookbook contains a wide variety of delicious crinkle cookie recipes.

Chocolate Crinkle Cookies

Ingredients:

2 cups white sugar
1 cup unsweetened cocoa powder
1/2 cup vegetable oil
4 large eggs
2 tsps. vanilla extract
2 cups all-purpose flour
2 tsps. baking powder
1/2 tsp. salt
1/2 cup confectioners' sugar

Directions:

1. Mix sugar, cocoa, and oil together in a medium bowl.
2. Beat in eggs, one at a time, until combined.
3. Stir in vanilla.
4. Combine flour, baking powder, and salt in another bowl.
5. Gradually stir dry ingredients into the wet ingredients until thoroughly mixed.
6. Cover dough and refrigerator for at least 4 hours.
7. Preheat the oven to 350 degrees F (175 degrees C).
8. Line two baking sheets with parchment paper.
9. Roll or scoop chilled dough into 1-inch balls.
10. Coat each ball in confectioners' sugar and place 1 inch apart on the prepared cookie sheets.
11. Bake in the preheated oven for 10 to 12 minutes.
12. Let stand on the cookie sheet for a few minutes before transferring to wire racks to cool.
13. Repeat Steps 4 and 5 to make remaining batches.

Dark Mocha Crinkles

Ingredients:

1 cup butter, at room temperature
3/4 cup brown sugar
⅓ cup white sugar
1/4 cup instant coffee powder
2 eggs
1 tsp. vanilla extract
2 cups all-purpose flour
3/4 cup cocoa powder
1 tsp. baking soda
1/2 tsp. salt
1/2 cup white sugar
24 dark chocolate wafers

Directions:

1. Preheat the oven to 375 degrees F (190 degrees C).
2. Line 2 baking sheets with parchment paper.
3. Combine butter, brown sugar, 1/3 cup sugar, and coffee powder in a large bowl.
4. Beat with an electric mixer until creamy. Blend in eggs and vanilla extract.
5. Mix in flour, cocoa powder, baking soda, and salt together until dough is uniform.
6. Pour 1/2 cup sugar onto a shallow plate. Shape dough into 2-inch balls and roll in the sugar until coated.
7. Arrange on the prepared baking sheets.
8. Bake in the preheated oven until edges are set, about 10 minutes.
9. Immediately press a dark chocolate wafer into each cookie.
10. Let cool on a wire rack.

Fudgy Chocolate Crinkle Cookies

Ingredients:

1 cup white sugar
2 large eggs
3 tbsps. vegetable oil
1 tsp. vanilla extract
1/4 cup margarine, melted
1 cup all-purpose flour
9 tbsps. unsweetened cocoa powder
1 tsp. baking powder
1/4 tsp. salt
1 cup white chocolate chips
3 tbsps. white sugar

Directions:

1. Mix 1 cup sugar, eggs, oil, and vanilla together in a large bowl until well blended.
2. Stir in melted margarine.
3. Stir in flour, cocoa, baking powder, and salt.
4. Mix until well blended.
5. Stir in white chocolate chips.
6. Mix until well blended.
7. Cover and chill until dough is firm enough to shape into balls, about 1 hour.
8. Meanwhile, preheat the oven to 300 degrees F (150 degrees C).
9. Roll dough into 1 1/2-inch balls.
10. Roll balls in remaining 3 tbsps. sugar.
11. Place 2 inches apart on ungreased cookie sheets.
12. Bake in the preheated oven until crackled on top and slightly firm to the touch, about 20 minutes.
13. Cool on the baking sheet for 1 minute before removing to a wire rack to cool completely.

Chocolate-Peppermint Crinkle Cookies

Ingredients:

1 cup white sugar
1/2 cup unsweetened cocoa powder
1/4 cup vegetable oil
2 large eggs
3 tsps. peppermint extract, or more to taste
1 cup all-purpose flour
1 tsp. baking powder
1/4 tsp. salt
1/2 cup semisweet chocolate chips
1/4 cup confectioners' sugar

Directions:

1. Mix white sugar, cocoa, and vegetable oil together in a bowl.
2. Beat in eggs and peppermint extract.
3. Separately mix together flour, baking powder, and salt; combine with above ingredients.
4. Mix in chocolate chips.
5. Cover dough and place in a freezer for 1 hour (or refrigerate for 3 hours or longer.)
6. Preheat the oven to 350 degrees F (175 degrees C).
7. Line baking sheets with parchment paper.
8. Take dough out of the freezer and remove by rounded tbsps.
9. Form into balls with clean hands.
10. Roll each ball in confectioners' sugar and place on prepared baking sheets.
11. Bake in the preheated oven until a toothpick comes out mostly clean, about 20 minutes.

Vegan Chocolate Crinkle Cookies

Ingredients:

2 tbsps. ground flax seeds
⅔ cup water, divided
1 1/2 cups all-purpose flour
1/2 cup unsweetened cocoa powder
2 tsps. baking powder
1/4 tsp. salt
3/4 cup vegan chocolate chips
3 tbsps. coconut oil
3/4 cup white sugar
1 tsp. vanilla extract
1/2 cup confectioners' sugar

Directions:

1. Preheat oven to 325 degrees F (175 degrees C).
2. Line 2 baking sheets with parchment paper.
3. Mix ground flax seeds with 1/3 cup water in a bowl; let sit until thickened, about 10 minutes.
4. Sift flour, cocoa powder, baking powder, and salt into a bowl.
5. Melt chocolate chips and coconut oil in a microwave-safe glass or ceramic bowl in 15-second intervals, stirring after each melting, 1 to 2 minutes.
6. Let cool.
7. Beat flax seed mixture, remaining 1/3 cup water, sugar, and vanilla extract in a bowl with an electric mixer until creamy, about 3 minutes.
8. Add flour mixture and melted chocolate; mix until well combined. Shape dough into 1-inch balls.
9. Roll in confectioner's sugar and place on the prepared baking sheets.
10. Bake in the preheated oven until firm to the touch, 11 to 13 minutes.

Brown Sugar Chocolate Crinkle Cookies

Ingredients:

1 cup semisweet chocolate chips
1 cup packed brown sugar
1/2 cup vegetable oil
2 eggs
1 tsp. vanilla extract
1 cup all-purpose flour
1 tsp. baking powder
1/4 tsp. salt
1/2 cup chopped walnuts
1/2 cup sifted confectioners' sugar

Directions:

1. Melt the chocolate chips and combine with the brown sugar and vegetable oil.
2. Add the eggs one at a time and beat well.
3. Stir in the vanilla.
4. Combine the flour, baking powder and salt.
5. Add flour mixture to the chocolate mixture.
6. Stir in the chopped walnuts. Chill dough for a few hours.
7. Preheat oven to 350 degrees F (175 degrees C).
8. Grease baking sheets.
9. Drop teaspoonfuls of dough in confectioners' sugar and roll to coat.
10. Place cookies on the prepared baking sheets.
11. Bake at 350 degrees F (175 degrees C) for 10 to 12 minutes.
12. Let cookies cool on racks.

Easy Chocolate Crackled Cookies

Ingredients:

1 (18.25 oz.) package devil's food cake mix
1/2 cup butter flavored shortening
1 tbsp. water
2 eggs
1 cup confectioners' sugar

Directions:

1. Preheat oven to 375 degrees F (190 degrees C).
2. Grease cookie sheets.
3. In a medium bowl, beat together the shortening, water, and eggs.
4. Add the cake mix, and mix until smooth.
5. Roll the dough into walnut sized balls, and roll the balls in the confectioners' sugar.
6. Place cookies 2 inches apart on the prepared cookie sheets.
7. Bake for 10 minutes in the preheated oven.
8. These are best served the same day, as the confectioners' sugar becomes absorbed by the cookie giving it a pasty look.
9. This can be fixed by dusting the cookies with sugar again.

Raspberry Chocolate Crinkles

Ingredients:

1 1/2 cups freeze-dried raspberries, divided
2 cups white sugar
1 cup unsweetened cocoa powder (not Dutch-process)
1/2 cup vegetable oil
2 tsps. baking powder
1 tsp. vanilla extract
1/2 tsp. kosher salt
4 eggs
2 cups flour
1/2 cup confectioners' sugar

Directions:

1. Pulse 1 1/2 cups raspberries in a blender or food processor until reduced to a powder.
2. Put white sugar, cocoa powder, oil, baking powder, vanilla, salt, and 1/4 cup powdered raspberries in a large bowl.
3. Beat together with a mixer until well blended.
4. Mix in eggs 1 at a time, waiting until each addition is incorporated before adding the next.
5. Add flour; mix on low speed until incorporated.
6. Cover with plastic wrap. Chill 4 to 8 hours or overnight.
7. Preheat oven to 350 degrees F (175 degrees C).
8. Line a baking sheet with a silicone baking mat or parchment paper.
9. Put confectioners' sugar in a small bowl; put remaining powdered raspberries in another small bowl.
10. Roll walnut-size pieces of dough into a ball, then roll each ball partly in powdered raspberries and partly in powdered sugar.
11. Arrange on prepared sheet and bake until barely set and crackled on top, 10 to 12 minutes.
12. Cool on sheet 10 minutes.
13. Transfer to a wire rack to cool completely.

Lemon Crinkle Cookies

Ingredients:

1 1/2 cups all-purpose flour
1/4 tsp. baking powder
1/4 tsp. salt
1/8 tsp. baking soda
1 cup white sugar
1/2 cup butter, softened
1 egg
1 tsp. vanilla extract
1 tsp. lemon extract
1 lemon, zested and juiced
1 drop yellow food coloring, or as desired
3/4 cup powdered sugar

Directions:

1. Sift flour, baking powder, salt, and baking soda together in a medium bowl.
2. Set aside.
3. Beat sugar and butter together in a large bowl using a handheld electric mixer or a stand mixer with the paddle attachment until creamy.
4. Beat in egg, vanilla extract, lemon extract, lemon zest and juice, and yellow food coloring. Scrape down the sides of the bowl and mix once more, making sure everything is combined.
5. Add flour mixture and mix until just combined.
6. Cover bowl and refrigerate cookie dough for 1 hour.
7. Preheat the oven to 350 degrees F (175 degrees C).
8. Line a baking sheet with parchment paper or a silicone baking mat.
9. Scoop dough using a cookie scoop or spoon into roughly 1 1/2-inch rounds. Slightly flatten cookies to 1/2-inch thickness.
10. Pour powdered sugar into a shallow bowl.
11. Place flattened rounds in powdered sugar and cover until well coated.

12. Remove with a fork or spoon and place on the prepared baking sheet.
13. Bake in the preheated oven until cookies are no longer glossy and have a matte look, 12 to 15 minutes.
14. Remove from the oven and let cool on the baking sheet for 3 to 5 minutes before transferring to a wire rack to cool completely.

Easy Lemon Cookies

Ingredients:

1 (15.25 oz.) package lemon cake mix
2 large eggs
⅓ cup vegetable oil
1 tsp. lemon extract
⅓ cup confectioners' sugar for decoration

Directions:

1. Preheat the oven to 375 degrees F (190 degrees C).
2. Pour cake mix into a large bowl.
3. Stir in eggs, oil, and lemon extract until well blended.
4. Working in batches, drop teaspoonfuls of dough into a bowl of confectioners' sugar.
5. Roll dough in sugar until lightly coated, then place 2 inches apart onto ungreased cookie sheets.
6. Bake in the preheated oven until the bottoms are light brown, 6 to 9 minutes.

Lemon Whippersnappers

Ingredients:

1 (18.25 oz.) package lemon cake mix
2 cups frozen whipped topping, thawed
1 egg, beaten
1/2 cup confectioners' sugar

Directions:

1. In a large bowl combine cake mix, whipped topping and egg; mix until well combined. Chill the dough several hours or overnight (or freeze dough wrapped in plastic).
2. Preheat oven to 350 degrees F (175 degrees C).
3. Form tbsps. of dough into one-inch balls and roll them in the confectioners' sugar.
4. Place the cookies on greased or parchment lined cookie sheet a couple inches apart.
5. Bake 10 to 12 minutes until cookies are set, but not browned.
6. Cool on wire rack.

Cake Mix Crinkle Cookies

Ingredients:

1 (15.25 oz.) package white cake mix
2 large eggs
6 tbsps. unsalted butter, melted
1/2 cup powdered sugar

Directions:

1. Position a rack in the center of the oven and preheat to 375 degrees F (190 degrees C).
2. Stir cake mix, eggs, and butter together in a large bowl to form a soft cookie dough.
3. Shape dough into 1-inch balls; roll in powdered sugar to coat.
4. Set balls about 2 inches apart on ungreased baking sheets.
5. Bake in the preheated oven, one pan at a time, just until edges are firm and cracks appear slightly moist, 9 to 11 minutes.
6. Cool on pans for 3 minutes; transfer to a wire rack to cool completely.

Blueberry Crinkle Cookies

Cookies Ingredients:

1 cup frozen wild blueberries
2 cups all-purpose flour
1 tsp. baking powder
1/2 tsp. salt
1 cup white sugar
⅓ cup vegetable oil
2 large egg whites
1 tsp. lemon zest
1/2 tsp. vanilla extract

Crinkle Coating Ingredients:

1/2 cup white sugar, or as needed
1/2 cup powdered sugar, or as needed

Directions:

1. Place frozen blueberries in a microwave-safe bowl and microwave until defrosted, 1 to 2 minutes.
2. Allow to cool to room temperature, 3 to 5 minutes; do not drain.
3. Whisk flour, baking powder, and salt together in a small bowl until well combined.
4. Transfer cooled blueberries and juice to a large bowl.
5. Add sugar and oil and whisk until thoroughly combined.
6. Mix in egg whites, lemon zest, and vanilla until thoroughly incorporated.
7. Add flour mixture in 2 batches, mixing after each addition until just combined.
8. Cover and refrigerate for at least 2 hours.
9. Preheat the oven to 400 degrees F (200 degrees C).
10. Line 2 baking sheets with parchment paper.
11. Prepare coating ingredients by placing each sugar in a separate small bowl.
12. Remove dough from the refrigerator. Scoop 1 1/2 tbsps. dough and carefully shape into a ball (the dough will still be kind of soft and sticky.) Coat the ball in white sugar, then drop into powdered sugar and roll to thoroughly coat.

13. Place on a prepared baking sheet.
14. Repeat the process with the remaining dough, spacing cookies 1 1/2 inches apart on the baking sheets.
15. Bake in the preheated oven until cookies are just set, 8 to 10 minutes, switching racks halfway through.
16. Cool on the baking sheet briefly before removing to a wire rack to cool completely.

Molasses Crinkles

Ingredients:

3/4 cup shortening
1 cup packed brown sugar
1 egg
1/4 cup molasses
2 1/4 cups all-purpose flour
2 tsps. baking soda
1/4 tsp. salt
1/2 tsp. ground cloves
1 tsp. ground cinnamon
1 tsp. ground ginger
⅓ cup granulated sugar for decoration

Directions:

1. Cream the shortening and the brown sugar.
2. Stir in the egg and molasses and mix well.
3. Combine the flour, baking soda, salt, cloves, cinnamon, and ginger.
4. Add the flour mixture to the shortening mixture and mix well.
5. Cover and chill dough for at least 2 to 3 hours.
6. Preheat oven to 350 degrees F (175 degrees C).
7. Grease cookie sheets.
8. Roll dough into balls the size of large walnuts.
9. Roll balls in sugar and place 3 inches apart on the prepared baking sheets.
10. Bake at 350 degrees F (175 degrees C) for 10 to 12 minutes.
11. Let cool for one minute before transferring to a wire rack to continue cooling.

Ginger Crinkles

Ingredients:

⅔ cup vegetable oil
1 cup white sugar
1 egg
1/4 cup molasses
2 cups all-purpose flour
2 tsps. baking soda
1 tsp. ground cinnamon
1 tsp. ground ginger
1/4 cup white sugar
1/2 tsp. salt

Directions:

1. Mix oil and sugar thoroughly with electric mixer.
2. Add egg and mix well.
3. Pour in molasses. Sift and add dry ingredients until incorporated.
4. Roll teaspoonful of dough into ball, drop into sugar to coat.
5. Place on ungreased cookie sheet.
6. Bake at 350 degrees F (175 degrees C) for 15 minutes.

Raspberry Molasses Crinkles

3/4 cup butter flavored shortening
1 cup packed brown sugar
1/4 cup molasses
1 egg
2 1/4 cups all-purpose flour
2 tsps. baking soda
1 tsp. ground cinnamon
1 tsp. ground ginger
1/2 tsp. ground cloves
1/4 tsp. salt
⅓ cup white sugar
1/2 cup seedless raspberry jam

Directions:

1. Mix the butter-flavored shortening and brown sugar with an electric mixer in a large bowl until smooth, and add the molasses and egg.
2. Beat until fluffy, 2 to 3 minutes, and stir in the flour, baking soda, cinnamon, ginger, cloves and salt.
3. Form the dough into a ball, cover, and refrigerate at least 2 hours.
4. Preheat an oven to 350 degrees F (175 degrees C).
5. Line cookie sheets with parchment paper and set aside.
6. Place the sugar in a shallow bowl.
7. Cut the dough into 4 pieces, and cut each quarter into 12 small pieces.
8. Roll each piece into a 1 1/4 inch ball, and dip the balls into the sugar.
9. Place the cookies, sugar side up, onto the prepared baking sheets.
10. Using your thumb or the end of a wooden spoon, make an indentation in each cookie ball about 1/2 inch deep. Spoon 1/2 tsp. of raspberry jam into each thumbprint.
11. Bake in the preheated oven for 10 minutes, until the cookies are just set but not hard.
12. Let cool for 1 minute before transferring the cookies to a wire rack to finish cooling.

Molasses Peanut Butter Crinkles

Ingredients:

1 cup packed brown sugar
1/2 cup peanut butter
1/4 cup butter, softened
1/4 cup molasses
1 egg
2 cups all-purpose flour
2 tsps. baking soda
1/2 tsp. ground ginger
1/2 tsp. ground cloves
1/2 tsp. salt
⅓ cup granulated sugar for decoration

Directions:

1. Preheat oven to 375 degrees F (190 degrees C).
2. Mix together the brown sugar, peanut butter, butter, molasses and egg in a large bowl.
3. In a medium bowl, sift together the flour, baking soda, ginger, cloves and salt.
4. Add the dry ingredients to the wet ingredients and stir until well blended.
5. For each cookie, shape a generous tbsp. of dough into a ball and roll in granulated sugar.
6. Place the cookies 2 inches apart on an ungreased cookie sheet and bake for 10 minutes, or until just set.
7. Transfer to a wire rack to cool.

Easy Chocolate Crackled Cookies

Ingredients:

1 (18.25 oz.) package devil's food cake mix
1/2 cup butter flavored shortening
1 tbsp. water
2 eggs
1 cup confectioners' sugar

Directions:

1. Preheat oven to 375 degrees F (190 degrees C).
2. Grease cookie sheets.
3. In a medium bowl, beat together the shortening, water, and eggs.
4. Add the cake mix, and mix until smooth.
5. Roll the dough into walnut sized balls, and roll the balls in the confectioners' sugar.
6. Place cookies 2 inches apart on the prepared cookie sheets.
7. Bake for 10 minutes in the preheated oven. These are best served the same day, as the confectioners' sugar becomes absorbed by the cookie giving it a pasty look. This can be fixed by dusting the cookies with sugar again.

Cinnamon Sugar Crackle Cookies

Ingredients:

1 cup shortening
1-3/4 cups sugar, divided
2 large eggs, room temperature
2-3/4 cups all-purpose flour
2 tsps. cream of tartar
1 tsp. baking soda
1/2 tsp. salt
4 tsps. ground cinnamon

Directions:

1. Preheat oven to 400 degrees F.
2. In a large bowl, cream shortening and 1-1/2 cups sugar until light and fluffy.
3. Beat in eggs.
4. In another bowl, whisk flour, cream of tartar, baking soda and salt; gradually beat into creamed mixture.
5. In a small bowl, mix cinnamon and remaining sugar. Shape dough into 1-in. balls; roll in cinnamon sugar.
6. Place 2 in. apart on ungreased baking sheets.
7. Bake 8-10 minutes or until golden brown.
8. Cool 2 minutes before removing to wire racks to cool.

Mexican Crinkle Cookies

Ingredients:

3/4 cup butter, cubed
2 oz. unsweetened chocolate, chopped
1 cup packed brown sugar
1/4 cup light corn syrup
1 large egg, room temperature
2 cups all-purpose flour
2 tsps. baking soda
1-1/2 tsps. ground cinnamon, divided
1/4 tsp. salt
1/2 cup confectioners' sugar

Directions:

1. In a microwave, melt butter and chocolate; stir until smooth.
2. Beat in brown sugar and corn syrup until blended.
3. Beat in egg.
4. In another bowl, whisk flour, baking soda, 1 tsp. cinnamon and salt; gradually beat into brown sugar mixture.
5. Refrigerate, covered, until firm, about 1 hour.
6. Preheat oven to 350°.
7. In a shallow bowl, mix confectioners' sugar and remaining cinnamon. Shape dough into 1-1/2-in. balls; roll in confectioners' sugar mixture.
8. Place 2 in. apart on greased baking sheets.
9. Bake until cookies are set and tops are cracked, 10-12 minutes.
10. Cool on pans 2 minutes.
11. Remove to wire racks to finish cooling.

Fudgy Mint Crinkle Cookies

Ingredients:

1 package devil's food cake mix (regular size)
1/2 cup butter, softened
2 large eggs, room temperature
1 tbsp. water
2 tbsps. confectioners' sugar
2 packages (5 oz. each) chocolate-covered thin mint candies

Directions:

1. Preheat oven to 375 degrees F.
2. In a large bowl, mix cake mix, butter, eggs and water to form a soft dough. Shape dough into 1-in. balls; roll in confectioners' sugar.
3. Place 2 in. apart on ungreased baking sheets.
4. Bake until set, 8-10 minutes.
5. Immediately press a mint into center of each cookie.
6. Cool on pans 2 minutes.
7. Remove from pans to wire racks to cool.

Powered Molasses Crinkle Cookies

Ingredients:

2/3 cup plus 2 tbsps. sugar, divided
1/4 cup sunflower oil
1 large egg, room temperature
1/4 cup molasses
2 cups white whole wheat flour or whole wheat pastry flour
2 tsps. baking soda
1 tsp. ground cinnamon
1/2 tsp. salt
1/4 tsp. ground ginger
1/4 tsp. ground cloves
3 tbsps. confectioners' sugar

Directions:

1. Preheat oven to 375 degrees F.
2. In a large bowl, beat 2/3 cup sugar and sunflower oil until blended.
3. Beat in egg, then molasses.
4. In another bowl, whisk flour, baking soda, cinnamon, salt, ginger and cloves; gradually beat into sugar mixture.
5. Combine confectioners' sugar and remaining 2 Tbsp. sugar. Shape dough into 1-in. balls; roll in sugar mixture.
6. Place 1 in. apart on greased baking sheets.
7. Bake until edges are firm, 10-12 minutes.
8. Cool on pans 5 minutes.
9. Remove to wire racks to cool.
10. Store in an airtight container.

Red Velvet Crinkle Cookies

Ingredients:

1 cup butter, softened
2-1/2 cups sugar
4 large eggs, room temperature
2 tsps. white vinegar
2 tsps. red paste food coloring
1 tsp. vanilla extract
4 cups all-purpose flour
1/2 cup baking cocoa
3 tsps. baking powder
1/2 tsp. salt
1 cup white baking chips
Confectioners' sugar

Directions:

1. In a large bowl, cream butter and sugar until light and fluffy, 5-7 minutes.
2. Beat in eggs, 1 at a time.
3. Beat in vinegar, food coloring and vanilla.
4. In another bowl, whisk flour, cocoa, baking powder and salt; gradually beat into creamed mixture.
5. Stir in chips.
6. Refrigerate, covered, 1 hour or until firm.
7. Preheat oven to 350 degrees F. Shape dough into 1-1/2-in. balls; roll in confectioners' sugar.
8. Place 2 in. apart on parchment-lined baking sheets.
9. Bake until tops are cracked and edges are set, 12-15 minutes.
10. Cool on pans 5 minutes.
11. Remove to wire racks to cool.

Chipotle Crackle Cookies

Ingredients:

2 large eggs, room temperature
1 cup sugar
1/4 cup canola oil
2 tsps. vanilla extract
2 oz. unsweetened chocolate, melted and cooled
1 cup all-purpose flour
1 tbsp. toasted wheat germ
3/4 tsp. baking powder
1/4 tsp. salt
1/8 tsp. ground chipotle pepper
1/4 cup miniature semisweet chocolate chips
1/3 cup confectioners' sugar

Directions:

1. In a large bowl, beat eggs, sugar, oil and vanilla until combined.
2. Add melted chocolate.
3. Combine flour, wheat germ, baking powder, salt and chipotle pepper.
4. Gradually add to egg mixture and mix well.
5. Fold in chocolate chips.
6. Cover and refrigerate for 2 hours.
7. Preheat oven to 350°.
8. Place confectioners' sugar in a small bowl. Scoop dough using a 1-in. scoop; roll balls in confectioners' sugar.
9. Place 2 in. apart on baking sheets coated with cooking spray.
10. Bake 8-10 minutes or until set.
11. Remove to wire racks to cool.

Crisp Lemon Cake Mix Crackle Cookies

Ingredients:

1 (15.25 oz.) package lemon cake mix
1 cup crispy rice cereal (such as Rice Krispies®)
1 cup unsalted butter, melted
1 large egg, slightly beaten

Directions:

1. Preheat the oven to 350 degrees F (175 degrees C).
2. Blend cake mix, cereal, melted butter, and egg together in a bowl.
3. Form dough into 1-inch balls and place 2 inches apart on ungreased cookie sheets.
4. Bake in the preheated oven until golden brown around the edges, 9 to 12 minutes.
5. Cool for 1 minute before transferring from the cookie sheet to a wire rack to cool completely.

Gingerbread Gooey Butter Crinkle Cookies

Ingredients:

2 1/4 cups all-purpose flour
1 tbsp. all-purpose flour
2 1/2 tsps. ground ginger
2 tsps. baking powder
2 tsps. ground cinnamon
1/4 tsp. baking soda
1/2 tsp. ground allspice
1/2 tsp. ground nutmeg
1/4 tsp. ground cloves
1 (8 oz.) package cream cheese, softened
1 stick butter, softened
1 cup white sugar
1/2 cup firmly packed brown sugar
1 tbsp. molasses
1 tsp. vanilla extract
1/4 tsp. almond extract
1/2 tsp. salt
1 large egg
1 large egg yolk
1 1/2 cups confectioners' sugar

Directions:

1. Combine 2 1/4 cups plus 1 tbsp. flour, ginger, baking powder, cinnamon, baking soda, allspice, nutmeg, and ground cloves in a bowl.
2. Whisk to combine, then set aside.
3. Combine cream cheese and butter in the bowl of a stand mixer. Blend on medium-high speed until smooth and creamy.
4. Add white and brown sugar, molasses, vanilla extract, almond extract, and salt. Blend on medium-high speed until smooth.
5. Add in egg and egg yolk and blend again on medium speed, 1 to 2 minutes. Scrape down the sides as necessary.

6. Add the dry mixture slowly just until dough is blended, scraping down sides as necessary. Dough will be very soft.
7. Cover work bowl with plastic wrap and refrigerate for at least 2 hours, up to overnight, to allow dough to chill and firm.
8. Preheat the oven to 325 degrees F (165 degrees C).
9. Line baking sheets with Silpat® mat or parchment paper.
10. Roll dough into approximately walnut-sized balls.
11. Pour confectioners' sugar into a bowl and roll dough balls in the sugar until very well coated.
12. Set on the prepared baking sheet, leaving 1 1/2 to 2 inches of space in between, about 8 to 12 cookies per sheet, depending on how large you decide to make the cookies.
13. Bake in the preheated oven until the edges are just starting to firm and become golden browned and the center looks mostly set, 15 to 17 minutes.
14. Cool on baking sheet for 2 minutes before carefully transferring to a wire rack to cool. This should yield a chewy cookie with slightly crispy edges.
15. Repeat with remaining cookie dough.

Earthquake Cookies

Ingredients:

1 (18.25 oz.) package devil's food cake mix
2 eggs
1/2 cup shortening
3/4 cup confectioners' sugar
1 tbsp. water

Directions:

1. Mix cake mix, eggs, shortening, and water in medium size bowl.
2. Mix with a spoon. Chill for 1 hour.
3. Shape dough into balls, roll in powdered sugar.
4. Place on cookie sheet and bake at 375 degrees F (190 degrees C) for 8-10 minutes; or until brown.

Merry Grinchmas Cookies

Ingredients:

1/2 cup butter, softened
1 package (8 oz.) cream cheese, softened
1-1/4 cups sugar
2 tsps. vanilla extract
1 tsp. green food coloring
2 large eggs
3 cups all-purpose flour
2 tsps. baking powder
1/4 tsp. salt
1 cup confectioners' sugar
48 heart-shaped gumdrops

Directions:

1. In a large bowl, beat butter, cream cheese and sugar until smooth.
2. Beat in vanilla, food coloring and eggs, one at a time, beating well after each addition.
3. In another bowl, whisk together flour, baking powder and salt; gradually beat into creamed mixture.
4. Refrigerate, covered, 1 hour or until firm enough to shape.
5. Preheat oven to 350°. Shape dough into 1-1/2-in. balls; roll in confectioners' sugar.
6. Place 2 in. apart on ungreased baking sheets.
7. Bake until tops are cracked and edges are set, 12-15 minutes.
8. Immediately press a gumdrop into each cookie.
9. Cool cookies 5 minutes before removing to wire racks to cool.

Brownie Crackles

Ingredients:

1 package fudge brownie mix (13x9-inch pan size)
1 cup all-purpose flour
1 large egg, room temperature
1/2 cup water
1/4 cup canola oil
1 cup semisweet chocolate chips
Confectioners' sugar

Directions:

1. Preheat oven to 350 degrees F.
2. In a large bowl, beat brownie mix, flour, egg, water and oil until well blended.
3. Stir in chocolate chips.
4. Let stand 30 minutes.
5. Place confectioners' sugar in a shallow dish.
6. Drop dough by tablespoonfuls into sugar; gently roll to coat.
7. Place 2 in. apart on greased baking sheets.
8. Bake 8-10 minutes or until set.
9. Remove from pans to wire racks to cool.

Sprinkle Crinkle Cookies

Ingredients:

2 & 1/2 cups all-purpose flour
1 tsp. baking powder
1/2 tsp. salt
1/2 cup unsalted butter, softened
1 & 1/4 cups granulated sugar
2 large eggs
1 tsp. vanilla extract
1/3 cup multi-colored sprinkles
1/2 cup confectioners' sugar, sifted

Directions:

1. Whisk together the flour, baking powder, and salt.
2. Set aside.
3. Using an electric mixer on medium speed, beat the butter and sugar until light and fluffy.
4. Add the eggs, one at a time, mixing well after each addition.
5. Mix in the vanilla.
6. Reduce mixer speed to low.
7. Gradually add the flour mixture, mixing just until combined.
8. Stir in the sprinkles.
9. Refrigerate the dough for 30 minutes.
10. Preheat oven to 350 degrees F.
11. Line baking sheets with silicone liners or parchment paper.
12. Place the confectioners' sugar in a small bowl.
13. Using a tablespoonful of dough at a time (I use a #50 scoop), roll the chilled cookie dough into balls. Then roll each in confectioners' sugar, making sure to coat thoroughly.
14. Place cookies on the prepared pans, leaving about 2 inches between the cookies.
15. Bake, one pan at a time, 14 to 18 minutes, or until the edges are lightly browned. Do not over-bake.
16. Cool the cookies on the pan for 5 minutes. Then transfer them to a wire rack to cool completely.

Molasses Spice Crinkle

Ingredients:

2 cups all-purpose flour
1 tsp. baking powder
1 tsp. baking soda
1 tsp. ground ginger
1 tsp. ground cinnamon
1/2 tsp. ground nutmeg
1/4 tsp. salt
1/4 tsp. ground cloves
1/4 tsp. ground allspice
3/4 cup shortening
1 cup granulated sugar
1 egg
1/4 cup molasses
1 cup coarse white sparkling sugar

Directions:

1. In medium bowl, mix flour, baking powder, baking soda, ginger, cinnamon, nutmeg, salt, cloves and allspice; set aside.
2. In large bowl, beat shortening with electric mixer on medium speed until fluffy.
3. Gradually add granulated sugar, beating well.
4. Add egg and molasses; beat well.
5. Gradually add flour mixture, beating on low speed until blended.
6. Cover; refrigerate 1 hour.
7. Heat oven to 375 degrees F. Shape dough into 1-inch balls; roll in sparkling sugar. On ungreased cookie sheets, place balls 2 inches apart.
8. Bake 9 to 11 minutes (tops will crack) or just until set.
9. Remove from cookie sheets to cooling racks.

Cake Mix Fudge Crinkle Cookies

Ingredients:

1 box devil's food cake mix
1/3 cup vegetable oil
2 eggs
1 tsp. vanilla
Powdered sugar

Directions:

1. Heat oven to 350 degrees F (325 degrees F for dark or nonstick cookie sheets). In large bowl, stir dry cake mix, oil, eggs and vanilla with spoon until dough forms.
2. Refrigerate dough 15 to 30 minutes, or as needed for easier handling. Shape dough into 1-inch balls.
3. Roll balls in powdered sugar. On ungreased cookie sheets, place balls about 2 inches apart.
4. Bake 9 to 11 minutes or until set.
5. Cool 1 minute; remove from cookie sheets to cooling rack.
6. Cool completely, about 30 minutes.
7. Store tightly covered.

Chocolate Mint Thumbprint Christmas Crinkles

Ingredients:

2 cups all-purpose flour
1 cup unsweetened baking cocoa
2 tsps. baking powder
1/2 tsp. salt
2 cups granulated sugar
1/2 cup vegetable oil
4 large eggs
1 tsp. vanilla
1 tsp. peppermint extract
1/2 cup powdered sugar

Directions:

1. Mint or candy cane flavored Hershey's Kisses
2. In medium bowl, mix flour, baking cocoa, baking powder and salt; set aside.
3. In large bowl, beat granulated sugar, oil and eggs with whisk until well mixed.
4. Beat in vanilla and peppermint extract.
5. Stir dry ingredients into wet ingredients just until combined.
6. Cover bowl with plastic wrap, and refrigerate at least 2 hours.
7. Heat oven to 350 degrees F.
8. Line cookie sheets with cooking parchment paper.
9. Place powdered sugar in small bowl. Shape dough into tbsp.-size balls; roll in powdered sugar.
10. Place on cookie sheets about 1 1/2 inches apart.
11. Bake 10 to 12 minutes, until cookies crackle and dough doesn't look raw.
12. When cookies are done, immediately place a KISSES candy in center of each cookie, and press lightly.
13. Cool on cookie sheet 2 minutes.
14. Remove to cooling rack; cool completely until candy is set.

Vanilla Bean Sugar Cookie Crinkles

Ingredients:

3 cups all-purpose flour
2 tsps. baking powder
1/2 tsp. baking soda
1/2 tsp. salt
1 1/2 cups granulated sugar
1 cup butter, softened
2 vanilla beans, cut in half lengthwise, scraped
2 eggs
1 cup powdered sugar
Additional powdered sugar for sprinkling, if desired

Directions:

1. Heat oven to 325 degrees F. In small bowl, mix flour, baking powder, baking soda and salt; set aside.
2. In large bowl, beat granulated sugar, softened butter and seeds from 2 vanilla beans with electric mixer on medium speed about 1 minute or until fluffy; scrape side of bowl.
3. Beat in eggs, one at a time, just until smooth. On low speed, beat flour mixture into sugar mixture until well blended.
4. Cover and let dough stand at room temperature 10 minutes.
5. Shape dough into 60 (1 1/4-inch) balls. In small bowl, place 1 cup powdered sugar.
6. Roll each cookie in powdered sugar; shake off excess.
7. Place on ungreased cookie sheets 2 inches apart.
8. Bake 12 to 14 minutes or until edges are until light brown.
9. Cool 2 minutes; remove from cookie sheet to cooling rack.
10. Cool completely, at least 15 minutes.
11. Sprinkle with additional powdered sugar.
12. Store in airtight container at room temperature.

Espresso Crinkles

Ingredients:

4 1/2 oz. all-purpose flour (about 1 cup)
1 1/4 cups powdered sugar, divided
1/4 cup unsweetened cocoa
1 1/4 tsps. baking powder
1/8 tsp. salt
5 1/4 tsps. canola oil
1 1/2 oz. unsweetened chocolate, chopped
1 tsp. instant espresso granules
3/4 cup packed brown sugar
3 tbsps. light-colored corn syrup
1 1/2 tsps. vanilla extract
2 large egg whites

Directions:

1. Weigh or lightly spoon flour into dry measuring cups; level with a knife.
2. Combine flour, 3/4 cup powdered sugar, cocoa, baking powder, and salt in a medium bowl; stir with a whisk.
3. Combine oil and chocolate in a small saucepan over low heat; cook until chocolate melts, stirring constantly.
4. Add espresso granules to pan; stir until blended.
5. Remove from heat.
6. Pour chocolate mixture into a large bowl; cool 5 minutes.
7. Stir in brown sugar, syrup, and vanilla.
8. Add egg whites, stirring with a whisk.
9. Add flour mixture to egg mixture, stirring gently just until combined.
10. Cover; chill at least 2 hours or overnight.
11. Preheat oven to 350°.
12. Roll dough into 1-inch balls. Dredge balls in remaining 1/2 cup powdered sugar; place balls 2 inches apart on 2 baking sheets lined with parchment paper.
13. Bake at 350 degrees F for 10 minutes or until tops are cracked and almost set.
14. Cool cookies on pan 2 minutes or until set; remove from pan.
15. Cool cookies on a wire rack.

Midnight Espresso Crinkles

Ingredients:

6 oz unsweetened baking chocolate, cut into small pieces
3/4 cup butter or margarine, softened
1/4 cup vegetable oil
1 cup granulated sugar
1 cup packed brown sugar
2 eggs
2 tbsps. instant coffee or espresso coffee granules
2 tbsps. water
1 tsp. vanilla
2 cups all-purpose flour
2 tsps. baking powder
1/2 tsp. salt
1/2 cup dark chocolate chips (from 12-oz bag)
1/4 cup decorator sugar crystals

Directions:

1. In small microwavable bowl, microwave baking chocolate uncovered on High 1 minute.
2. Stir; microwave 1 minute longer, stirring every 15 seconds, until melted and smooth.
3. In large bowl, beat butter, oil, granulated sugar and brown sugar with electric mixer on medium speed, scraping bowl occasionally, until light and fluffy.
4. Beat in melted chocolate and eggs until well blended.
5. In small bowl, dissolve coffee granules in water.
6. Add coffee mixture and vanilla to batter; beat until well blended. On low speed, beat in flour, baking powder and salt.
7. Stir in chocolate chips.
8. Cover with plastic wrap; refrigerate 30 minutes for easier handling.
9. Heat oven to 350 degrees F.
10. Place sugar crystals in small bowl. Shape dough by rounded tablespoonfuls into 1 1/2-inch balls; dip tops of balls in sugar. On ungreased cookie sheets, place balls, sugar sides up, 3 inches apart.

11. Bake 11 to 13 minutes or until tops look dry (do not overbake).
12. Cool 5 minutes; remove from cookie sheets to cooling racks.

Red Velvet Crackle Sandwich Cookies

Ingredients:

3 oz. semisweet baking chocolate, chopped
1/4 cup unsalted butter
1 cup granulated sugar
2 large eggs
1 tbsp. red liquid food coloring
2 cups all-purpose flour
2 tbsps. unsweetened cocoa
1 tsp. baking powder
1/2 tsp. baking soda
1/2 tsp. kosher salt
2 cups powdered sugar, divided
4 oz. cream cheese, softened

Directions:

1. Preheat oven to 375 degrees F with oven racks in the top third and bottom third of oven.
2. Melt chocolate and butter in a large microwave-safe glass bowl on medium (50% power) until melted and smooth, about 1 1/2 minutes, stirring every 30 seconds.
3. Whisk in granulated sugar, eggs, and food coloring until smooth.
4. Whisk together flour, cocoa, baking powder, baking soda, and salt, and add to butter mixture, stirring gently just to combine.
5. Place 1 cup of the powdered sugar in a small bowl.
6. Drop dough by tablespoonfuls into powdered sugar, rolling to coat, and place 1 inch apart on parchment-lined baking sheets.
7. Using the heal of your hand, gently flatten domed tops of dough.
8. Bake in preheated oven until cookies are almost set and outsides are crackled, 10 to 11 minutes.
9. Transfer pans to wire racks, and cool cookies completely, about 30 minutes.
10. Beat cream cheese and remaining 1 cup powdered sugar with an electric mixer on medium speed until smooth.

11. Spread 1 1/2 tsps. cream cheese filling onto flat side of half of the cookies.
12. Cover with remaining half of cookies, flat side down, and gently press.

Snow Crackle Cookies

Ingredients:

8 (1 oz) squares chopped semi-sweet chocolate
1 1/3 cups all-purpose flour
1/2 cup dark chocolate cocoa powder
2 tsps. baking powder
1/8 tsp. salt
1/2 cup softened butter
1 1/2 cups divided granulated sugar
1 cup firmly packed dark brown sugar
2 large eggs
1/2 tsp. orange extract
1/3 cup milk
1 cup confectioner's sugar

Directions:

1. In a small bowl, microwave chocolate on high, in 30-second intervals, stirring between each, until chocolate is melted and smooth, about 90-seconds total.
2. In a medium bowl, add flour, cocoa powder, baking powder and salt, whisk together.
3. In a large bowl, add butter, Â1/2 cup sugar and brown sugar.
4. Using a handheld mixer at medium speed, beat the butter and sugars until fluffy, about 3-4 minutes.
5. Add the eggs to the mixture, beating in one at a time, beat in orange extract.
6. Add flour mixture alternately with milk, beginning and ending with flour mixture.
7. Cover and chill dough for 2 hours in refrigerator.
8. Preheat oven to 350 degrees F.
9. Prepare 2 baking sheets with parchment.
10. In a small bowl, add remaining 1 cup granulated sugar.
11. In another small bowl, add confectioners' sugar.
12. Using a cookie scoop, drop dough 2 tbsps. at a time into granulated sugar and roll until coated.
13. Place 2 inches apart on prepared cookie sheets.
14. Repeat with remaining dough.

15. Bake for 15-17 minutes or until surface is cracked and edges look dry.
16. Cool completely on wire racks. Dust with confectioners' sugar.

Double Ginger Crackle Cookies

Ingredients:

3⁄4 cup shortening
1 cup sugar
1 large egg
1⁄4 cup molasses
2 cups all-purpose flour
2 tsps. baking soda
1⁄4 tsp. salt
1⁄2 cup finely chopped candied ginger
1 tbsp. ground ginger
1 tsp. cinnamon
1 tsp. clove
Granulated sugar, to roll dough balls in

Directions:

1. Cream together shortening and sugar.
2. Add egg and molasses and mix well.
3. Stir together the flour, soda, salt, spices and candied ginger. Blend into the creamed mixture.
4. Shape into balls about 1-inch in diameter.
5. Roll balls in granulated sugar.
6. Place about 2-inches apart on greased cookie sheets.
7. Bake at 350 degrees F for 8-10 minutes or until golden. Careful not to overbake.
8. Cookies should be slightly soft when removed from the oven.
9. Allow to cool on cookie sheet for a few minutes before removing to racks to complete cooling.

Brown Sugar Crackle Cookies

Ingredients:

3 cups all-purpose flour
1/2 tsp. baking soda
1/2 tsp. salt
1 cup butter, softened
2 cups packed brown sugar
2 eggs
1 tbsp. vanilla
3/4 cup coarse white sparkling sugar

Directions:

1. Heat oven to 350 degrees F. In medium bowl, mix flour, baking soda and salt; set aside.
2. In large bowl, beat butter and brown sugar with electric mixer on medium speed about 1 minute or until fluffy; scrape side of bowl.
3. Beat in eggs, one at a time, just until smooth.
4. Beat in vanilla. On low speed, gradually beat flour mixture into butter mixture until well blended.
5. Shape dough into 56 (1 1/2-inch) balls.
6. Roll in sparkling sugar.
7. Place 2 inches apart on ungreased cookie sheet.
8. Bake 10 to 13 minutes or until edges are light golden brown.
9. Cool on cookie sheet 2 minutes; remove from cookie sheet to cooling rack.
10. Cool completely, about 15 minutes.
11. Store in airtight container at room temperature.

Chocolate Toffee Crinkle Cookies

Ingredients:

8 oz. semisweet baking chocolate, chopped
1/4 cup butter or margarine, cut up
1 1/4 cups all-purpose flour
1/4 cup unsweetened baking cocoa
1/2 tsp. baking soda
1/4 tsp. salt
1 cup sugar
2 eggs
1 tsp. vanilla
1 bag (8 oz.) toffee bits
Sugar

Directions:

1. In 1-quart saucepan, heat chocolate and butter over medium-low heat, stirring frequently, until chocolate is melted and mixture is smooth; cool.
2. Heat oven to 350 degrees F.
3. Grease or line cookie sheets with cooking parchment paper.
4. In medium bowl, stir together flour, cocoa, baking soda and salt; set aside.
5. In large bowl, beat 1 cup sugar, the eggs and vanilla with electric mixer on medium speed 2 minutes or until well blended.
6. Add cooled chocolate mixture; beat on low speed until combined. Slowly beat in flour mixture until soft dough forms.
7. Stir in toffee bits.
8. Shape dough into 1 1/4-inch balls.
9. Onto ungreased cookie sheets, place balls 2 inches apart.
10. With bottom of glass dipped in sugar, flatten slightly.
11. Bake 8 to 10 minutes or until tops are dry (cookies will be soft in center).
12. Cool 3 minutes; remove from cookie sheets to cooling racks.
13. Cool completely before storing in airtight container.

Zebra Crinkles

Ingredients:

2 cups granulated sugar
1/2 cup vegetable oil
2 tsps. vanilla
4 oz. unsweetened baking chocolate, melted and cooled
4 eggs
2 cups all-purpose flour
2 tsps. baking powder
1/2 tsp. salt
1 cup powdered sugar
6 dozen Hershey's Hugs chocolates, unwrapped

Directions:

1. Mix granulated sugar, oil, vanilla and chocolate in large bowl.
2. Stir in eggs, one at a time.
3. Stir in flour, baking powder and salt.
4. Cover and refrigerate at least 3 hours.
5. Heat oven to 350 degrees F.
6. Grease cookie sheet.
7. Drop dough by teaspoonfuls into powdered sugar; roll in sugar to coat. Shape dough into balls.
8. Place about 2 inches apart on cookie sheet.
9. Bake 10 to 12 minutes or until almost no indentation remains when touched.
10. Immediately press 1 chocolate candy in center of each cookie.
11. Remove from cookie sheet.
12. Cool completely on cooling rack.

Hazelnut Crinkles

Ingredients:

3/4 cup granulated sugar
3/4 cup Nutella hazelnut spread with cocoa
1/2 cup butter or margarine, softened
1/2 tsp. vanilla
1 egg
1 3/4 cups all-purpose flour
1 tsp. baking soda
1/4 tsp. salt
3 tbsps. white decorator sugar crystals or granulated sugar

Directions:

1. Heat oven to 375 degrees F. In large bowl, beat granulated sugar, hazelnut spread, butter, vanilla and egg with electric mixer on medium speed, or mix with spoon.
2. Stir in flour, baking soda and salt.
3. Shape dough by rounded teaspoonfuls into 1-inch balls.
4. Roll in sugar crystals.
5. Place about 2 inches apart on ungreased cookie sheet.
6. Bake cookies 7 to 9 minutes or until puffed and edges are set.
7. Cool on cookie sheet 1 minute.
8. Remove from cookie sheet to wire rack; cool.

Hazelnut Cappuccino Crinkles

Ingredients:

1 pouch (1 lb. 1.5 oz.) double chocolate chunk cookie mix
3 tbsps. vegetable oil
2 tbsps. hazelnut-flavored syrup
2 tsps. instant coffee granules or crystals
1 egg
1/2 cup powdered sugar
30 coffee bean chocolate pieces

Directions:

1. Heat oven to 375 degrees F. In large bowl, stir cookie mix, oil, syrup, instant coffee and egg until soft dough forms.
2. Roll dough into 1-inch balls; roll in powdered sugar.
3. Place 2 inches apart onto ungreased cookie sheet.
4. Bake about 9 minutes or until set.
5. Immediately press candy piece into top of each cookie.
6. Cool 1 minute; remove from cookie sheet to wire rack.

Spiced Almond-Chocolate Crinkles

Ingredients:

1/4 cup butter or margarine
4 oz unsweetened baking chocolate, chopped
4 eggs
2 cups all-purpose flour
2 cups granulated sugar
1/2 cup chopped almonds
2 tsps. baking powder
1/2 tsp. salt
1/2 tsp. ground ginger
1/2 tsp. ground cinnamon
1/4 tsp. ground cloves
3/4 cup powdered sugar

Directions:

1. In 3-quart saucepan, melt butter and chocolate over low heat, stirring constantly, until smooth.
2. Remove from heat.
3. Cool slightly, about 5 minutes.
4. With spoon, beat eggs into chocolate mixture until well blended.
5. Beat in remaining ingredients except powdered sugar until well blended.
6. Cover dough with plastic wrap; refrigerate at least 1 hour for easier handling.
7. Heat oven to 300 degrees F.
8. Spray cookie sheets with cooking spray.
9. Place powdered sugar in small bowl. Shape dough into 1-inch balls; roll in powdered sugar, coating heavily. On cookie sheets, place balls 2 inches apart.
10. Bake 13 to 18 minutes or until set.
11. Immediately remove from cookie sheets to cooling racks.

Chocolate Crinkle Nests

Cake Mix Fudge Crinkle Cookies Ingredients:

1 box devil's food cake mix
1/3 cup vegetable oil
2 eggs
1 tsp. vanilla
Powdered sugar

Cake Mix Fudge Crinkle Cookies Directions:

1. Heat oven to 350 degrees F (325 degrees F for dark or nonstick cookie sheets). In large bowl, stir dry cake mix, oil, eggs and vanilla with spoon until dough forms.
2. Refrigerate dough 15 to 30 minutes, or as needed for easier handling. Shape dough into 1-inch balls.
3. Roll balls in powdered sugar. On ungreased cookie sheets, place balls about 2 inches apart.
4. Bake 9 to 11 minutes or until set.
5. Cool 1 minute; remove from cookie sheets to cooling rack.
6. Cool completely, about 30 minutes.
7. Store tightly covered.

Nest Ingredients:

1 cup sweetened coconut
1 bag candy-coated chocolate eggs
Green food coloring
Quart-sized plastic zip-top bag
Mixing bowls
Measuring cups
Tbsp.
Cookie sheet
Cooling rack

Nest Directions:

1. In quart-sized plastic zip-top bag, combine shredded coconut and two to three drops of green food coloring.
2. Seal bag and shake to combine, adding more coloring a drop at a time until desired color of green is reached.

3. Set aside, assemble your other ingredients and preheat the oven to 350 degrees.
4. Prepare Cake Mix Fudge Crinkle Cookie dough and refrigerate 15-30 minutes, until firm. Once dough has firmed up, using a tbsp., scoop and roll into 1 1/2-inch balls.
5. Coat each dough ball in powdered sugar.
6. On ungreased cookie sheets, place balls about 2 inches apart.
7. Pop in oven and bake 9 to 11 minutes or until set.
8. Cool two minutes, then, working quickly, make thumbprint indentations.
9. Fill each indentation with a sprinkling of tinted coconut, about 1 tbsp. per cookie.
10. Fill each coconut "nest" with three candy-coated chocolate eggs.
11. Carefully remove cookies from cookie sheet to cooling rack and cool completely.
12. Tip: Jelly beans or pastel malted milk balls would also make good "eggs"

Vanilla Cake Mix Crinkle Cookies

Ingredients:

1 box vanilla cake mix
2 eggs
1/3 cup vegetable oil
1/2 cup powdered icing sugar

Directions:

1. Preheat oven to 350 degrees F.
2. Line two baking sheets with parchment paper or silicone baking mats.
3. Set aside.
4. In a large bowl, beat together the cake mix, eggs and vegetable oil until smooth and completely combined, about 2 minutes.
5. Use a 1 1/2 tbsp. cookie scoop to portion out the cookie batter, then roll into balls.
6. Place each ball of dough individually in the powdered icing sugar and toss to coat completely.
7. Place each sugar-coated dough ball at least 3" apart on the prepared cookie sheets.
8. Bake for 10 minutes until lightly golden and spread out.
9. Allow the cookies to cool for 5 minutes on the baking sheet before attempting to remove to a cooling rack or serve.

Cinnamon Vanilla Crinkle Cookies

Cookie Dough Ingredients:

1 cup all-purpose flour
1 cup powdered sugar
3/4 tsp. baking powder
1/2 cup butter softened
1/2 tsp. vanilla extract
3/4 tsp. cinnamon powder
1/4 tsp. salt

Cinnamon Sugar Mix Ingredients:

1/4 cup powdered sugar or as needed
1/8 tsp. cinnamon powder

Cookie Dough Directions:

1. In a large bowl, mix together the following dry ingredients for the cookie dough – flour, cinnamon powder and salt until the ingredients are well mixed evenly.
2. In a different bowl, mix together the butter and powdered sugar (one cup) until sugar is dissolved.
3. Also add the vanilla extract and mix with the butter sugar mixture.
4. Pour the prepared butter sugar mixture to the dry flour mixture and mix well using a spoon to form a crumbly mixture.
5. Then knead with your hands to make the cinnamon cookie dough. In case the mixture is still crumbly and you have difficulty forming the dough, you may add about one tsp. of water or milk and knead again to make the cookie dough.
6. Cover the cookie dough and place the cookie dough for about 10 minutes in the refrigerator.
7. To make the cinnamon sugar mix for rolling the cookies:
8. In a bowl, mix together the 1/4 cup powdered sugar and also 1/2 tsp. cinnamon powder until they are evenly mixed.
9. Keep this mixture aside until the cookie dough is chilled and we are ready to bake the cookies.

Cinnamon Sugar Cookies Directions:

1. Preheat oven to 350 degrees F.
2. Layer a baking sheet with parchment paper.
3. Make small balls out of the prepared cookie dough (chilled dough) and roll the balls in the cinnamon sugar mix that we made.
4. Place the cookie dough balls in the baking sheet, make sure to leave some space between the cookie dough balls as they will expand while baking.
5. For best results, roll each of the cookies once more in the powdered sugar & cinnamon mix so they will have more coating which will help in creating beautiful crinkle patterns!
6. Bake the cookies in the preheated oven for about 14 to 15 minutes until they are lightly browned on the edges.
7. The cookies may look too soft at this point, but it's fine as they will harden enough as they cool down. If you bake for more time, the cookies can turn hard.
8. So once they are baked, immediately transfer the cookies from the hot oven.
9. Allow the cookies to cool down and enjoy.

Espresso Crinkles

Ingredients:

4 1/2 oz. all-purpose flour (about 1 cup)
1 1/4 cups powdered sugar, divided
1/4 cup unsweetened cocoa
1 1/4 tsps. baking powder
1/8 tsp. salt
5 1/4 tsps. canola oil
1 1/2 oz. unsweetened chocolate, chopped
1 tsp. instant espresso granules
3/4 cup packed brown sugar
3 tbsps. light-colored corn syrup
1 1/2 tsps. vanilla extract
2 large egg whites

Directions:

1. Weigh or lightly spoon flour into dry measuring cups; level with a knife.
2. Combine flour, 3/4 cup powdered sugar, cocoa, baking powder, and salt in a medium bowl; stir with a whisk.
3. Combine oil and chocolate in a small saucepan over low heat; cook until chocolate melts, stirring constantly.
4. Add espresso granules to pan; stir until blended.
5. Remove from heat.
6. Pour chocolate mixture into a large bowl; cool 5 minutes.
7. Stir in brown sugar, syrup, and vanilla.
8. Add egg whites, stirring with a whisk.
9. Add flour mixture to egg mixture, stirring gently just until combined.
10. Cover; chill at least 2 hours or overnight.
11. Preheat oven to 350°.
12. Roll dough into 1-inch balls. Dredge balls in remaining 1/2 cup powdered sugar; place balls 2 inches apart on 2 baking sheets lined with parchment paper.
13. Bake at 350° for 10 minutes or until tops are cracked and almost set.
14. Cool cookies on pan 2 minutes or until set; remove from pan.
15. Cool cookies on a wire rack.

Midnight Espresso Crinkles

Ingredients:

6 oz unsweetened baking chocolate, cut into small pieces
3/4 cup butter or margarine, softened
1/4 cup vegetable oil
1 cup granulated sugar
1 cup packed brown sugar
2 eggs
2 tbsps. instant coffee or espresso coffee granules
2 tbsps. water
1 tsp. vanilla
2 cups all-purpose flour
2 tsps. baking powder
1/2 tsp. salt
1/2 cup dark chocolate chips (from 12-oz bag)
1/4 cup decorator sugar crystals

Directions:

1. In small microwavable bowl, microwave baking chocolate uncovered on High 1 minute.
2. Stir; microwave 1 minute longer, stirring every 15 seconds, until melted and smooth.
3. In large bowl, beat butter, oil, granulated sugar and brown sugar with electric mixer on medium speed, scraping bowl occasionally, until light and fluffy.
4. Beat in melted chocolate and eggs until well blended.
5. In small bowl, dissolve coffee granules in water.
6. Add coffee mixture and vanilla to batter; beat until well blended. On low speed, beat in flour, baking powder and salt.
7. Stir in chocolate chips.
8. Cover with plastic wrap; refrigerate 30 minutes for easier handling.
9. Heat oven to 350 degrees F.
10. Place sugar crystals in small bowl. Shape dough by rounded tablespoonfuls into 1 1/2-inch balls; dip tops of balls in sugar. On ungreased cookie sheets, place balls, sugar sides up, 3 inches apart.

11. Bake 11 to 13 minutes or until tops look dry (do not overbake).
12. Cool 5 minutes; remove from cookie sheets to cooling racks.

Red Velvet Crackle Sandwich Cookies

Ingredients:

3 oz. semisweet baking chocolate, chopped
1/4 cup unsalted butter
1 cup granulated sugar
2 large eggs
1 tbsp. red liquid food coloring
2 cups all-purpose flour
2 tbsps. unsweetened cocoa
1 tsp. baking powder
1/2 tsp. baking soda
1/2 tsp. kosher salt
2 cups powdered sugar, divided
4 oz. cream cheese, softened

Directions:

1. Preheat oven to 375 degrees F with oven racks in the top third and bottom third of oven.
2. Melt chocolate and butter in a large microwave-safe glass bowl on medium (50% power) until melted and smooth, about 1 1/2 minutes, stirring every 30 seconds.
3. Whisk in granulated sugar, eggs, and food coloring until smooth.
4. Whisk together flour, cocoa, baking powder, baking soda, and salt, and add to butter mixture, stirring gently just to combine.
5. Place 1 cup of the powdered sugar in a small bowl.
6. Drop dough by tablespoonfuls into powdered sugar, rolling to coat, and place 1 inch apart on parchment-lined baking sheets.
7. Using the heal of your hand, gently flatten domed tops of dough.
8. Bake in preheated oven until cookies are almost set and outsides are crackled, 10 to 11 minutes.
9. Transfer pans to wire racks, and cool cookies completely, about 30 minutes.
10. Beat cream cheese and remaining 1 cup powdered sugar with an electric mixer on medium speed until smooth.

11. Spread 1 1/2 tsps. cream cheese filling onto flat side of half of the cookies.
12. Cover with remaining half of cookies, flat side down, and gently press.

Snow Crackle Cookies

Ingredients:

8 (1 oz) squares chopped semi-sweet chocolate
1 1/3 cups all-purpose flour
1/2 cup dark chocolate cocoa powder
2 tsps. baking powder
1/8 tsp. salt
1/2 cup softened butter
1 1/2 cups divided granulated sugar
1 cup firmly packed dark brown sugar
2 large eggs
1/2 tsp. orange extract
1/3 cup milk
1 cup confectioner's sugar

Directions:

1. In a small bowl, microwave chocolate on high, in 30-second intervals, stirring between each, until chocolate is melted and smooth, about 90 seconds total.
2. In a medium bowl, add flour, cocoa powder, baking powder and salt, whisk together.
3. In a large bowl, add butter, Â1/2 cup sugar and brown sugar.
4. Using a handheld mixer at medium speed, beat the butter and sugars until fluffy, about 3-4 minutes.
5. Add the eggs to the mixture, beating in one at a time, beat in orange extract.
6. Add flour mixture alternately with milk, beginning and ending with flour mixture.
7. Cover and chill dough for 2 hours in refrigerator.
8. Preheat oven to 350 degrees F.
9. Prepare 2 baking sheets with parchment.
10. In a small bowl, add remaining 1 cup granulated sugar.
11. In another small bowl, add confectioners' sugar.
12. Using a cookie scoop, drop dough 2 tbsps. at a time into granulated sugar and roll until coated.
13. Place 2 inches apart on prepared cookie sheets.
14. Repeat with remaining dough.

15. Bake for 15-17 minutes or until surface is cracked and edges look dry.
16. Cool completely on wire racks. Dust with confections' sugar.

Double Ginger Crackle Cookies

Ingredients:

3⁄4 cup shortening
1 cup sugar
1 large egg
1⁄4 cup molasses
2 cups all-purpose flour
2 tsps. baking soda
1⁄4 tsp. salt
1⁄2 cup finely chopped candied ginger
1 tbsp. ground ginger
1 tsp. cinnamon
1 tsp. clove
Granulated sugar, to roll dough balls in

Directions:

1. Cream together shortening and sugar; add egg and molasses and mix well.
2. Stir together the flour, soda, salt, spices and candied ginger.
3. Blend into the creamed mixture.
4. Shape into balls about 1-inch in diameter.
5. Roll balls in granulated sugar.
6. Place about 2-inches apart on greased cookie sheets.
7. Bake at 350 degrees F for 8-10 minutes or until golden. Careful not to overbake.
8. Cookies should be slightly soft when removed from the oven.
9. Allow to cool on cookie sheet for a few minutes before removing to racks to complete cooling.

Brown Sugar Crackle Cookies

Ingredients:

3 cups all-purpose flour
1/2 tsp. baking soda
1/2 tsp. salt
1 cup butter, softened
2 cups packed brown sugar
2 eggs
1 tbsp. vanilla
3/4 cup coarse white sparkling sugar

Directions:

1. Heat oven to 350 degrees F. In medium bowl, mix flour, baking soda and salt; set aside.
2. In large bowl, beat butter and brown sugar with electric mixer on medium speed about 1 minute or until fluffy; scrape side of bowl.
3. Beat in eggs, one at a time, just until smooth.
4. Beat in vanilla. On low speed, gradually beat flour mixture into butter mixture until well blended.
5. Shape dough into 56 (1 1/2-inch) balls.
6. Roll in sparkling sugar.
7. Place 2 inches apart on ungreased cookie sheet.
8. Bake 10 to 13 minutes or until edges are light golden brown.
9. Cool on cookie sheet 2 minutes; remove from cookie sheet to cooling rack.
10. Cool completely, about 15 minutes.
11. Store in airtight container at room temperature.

Chocolate Toffee Crinkle Cookies

Ingredients:

8 oz. semisweet baking chocolate, chopped
1/4 cup butter or margarine, cut up
1 1/4 cups all-purpose flour
1/4 cup unsweetened baking cocoa
1/2 tsp. baking soda
1/4 tsp. salt
1 cup sugar
2 eggs
1 tsp. vanilla
1 bag (8 oz.) toffee bits
Sugar

Directions:

1. In 1-quart saucepan, heat chocolate and butter over medium-low heat, stirring frequently, until chocolate is melted and mixture is smooth; cool.
2. Heat oven to 350 degrees F.
3. Grease or line cookie sheets with cooking parchment paper.
4. In medium bowl, stir together flour, cocoa, baking soda and salt; set aside.
5. In large bowl, beat 1 cup sugar, the eggs and vanilla with electric mixer on medium speed 2 minutes or until well blended.
6. Add cooled chocolate mixture; beat on low speed until combined. Slowly beat in flour mixture until soft dough forms.
7. Stir in toffee bits.
8. Shape dough into 1 1/4-inch balls.
9. Onto ungreased cookie sheets, place balls 2 inches apart.
10. With bottom of glass dipped in sugar, flatten slightly.
11. Bake 8 to 10 minutes or until tops are dry (cookies will be soft in center).
12. Cool 3 minutes; remove from cookie sheets to cooling racks.
13. Cool completely before storing in airtight container.

Zebra Crinkles

Ingredients:

2 cups granulated sugar
1/2 cup vegetable oil
2 tsps. vanilla
4 oz. unsweetened baking chocolate, melted and cooled
4 eggs
2 cups all-purpose flour
2 tsps. baking powder
1/2 tsp. salt
1 cup powdered sugar
6 dozen Hershey's Hugs chocolates, unwrapped

Directions:

1. Mix granulated sugar, oil, vanilla and chocolate in large bowl.
2. Stir in eggs, one at a time.
3. Stir in flour, baking powder and salt.
4. Cover and refrigerate at least 3 hours.
5. Heat oven to 350 degrees F.
6. Grease cookie sheet.
7. Drop dough by teaspoonfuls into powdered sugar; roll in sugar to coat. Shape dough into balls.
8. Place about 2 inches apart on cookie sheet.
9. Bake 10 to 12 minutes or until almost no indentation remains when touched.
10. Immediately press 1 chocolate candy in center of each cookie.
11. Remove from cookie sheet.
12. Cool completely on cooling rack.

Hazelnut Crinkles

Ingredients:

3/4 cup granulated sugar
3/4 cup Nutella hazelnut spread with cocoa
1/2 cup butter or margarine, softened
1/2 tsp. vanilla
1 egg
1 3/4 cups all-purpose flour
1 tsp. baking soda
1/4 tsp. salt
3 tbsps. white decorator sugar crystals or granulated sugar

Directions:

1. Heat oven to 375 degrees F.
2. In large bowl, beat granulated sugar, hazelnut spread, butter, vanilla and egg with electric mixer on medium speed, or mix with spoon.
3. Stir in flour, baking soda and salt.
4. Shape dough by rounded teaspoonfuls into 1-inch balls.
5. Roll in sugar crystals.
6. Place about 2 inches apart on ungreased cookie sheet.
7. Bake cookies 7 to 9 minutes or until puffed and edges are set.
8. Cool on cookie sheet 1 minute.
9. Remove from cookie sheet to wire rack; cool.

Hazelnut Cappuccino Crinkles

Ingredients:

1 pouch (1 lb. 1.5 oz.) double chocolate chunk cookie mix
3 tbsps. vegetable oil
2 tbsps. hazelnut-flavored syrup
2 tsps. instant coffee granules or crystals
1 egg
1/2 cup powdered sugar
30 coffee bean chocolate pieces

Directions:

1. Heat oven to 375 degrees F. In large bowl, stir cookie mix, oil, syrup, instant coffee and egg until soft dough forms.
2. Roll dough into 1-inch balls; roll in powdered sugar.
3. Place 2 inches apart onto ungreased cookie sheet.
4. Bake about 9 minutes or until set.
5. Immediately press candy piece into top of each cookie.
6. Cool 1 minute; remove from cookie sheet to wire rack.

Spiced Almond-Chocolate Crinkles

Ingredients:

1/4 cup butter or margarine
4 oz unsweetened baking chocolate, chopped
4 eggs
2 cups all-purpose flour
2 cups granulated sugar
1/2 cup chopped almonds
2 tsps. baking powder
1/2 tsp. salt
1/2 tsp. ground ginger
1/2 tsp. ground cinnamon
1/4 tsp. ground cloves
3/4 cup powdered sugar

Directions:

1. In 3-quart saucepan, melt butter and chocolate over low heat, stirring constantly, until smooth.
2. Remove from heat.
3. Cool slightly, about 5 minutes.
4. With spoon, beat eggs into chocolate mixture until well blended.
5. Beat in remaining ingredients except powdered sugar until well blended.
6. Cover dough with plastic wrap; refrigerate at least 1 hour for easier handling.
7. Heat oven to 300 degrees F.
8. Spray cookie sheets with cooking spray.
9. Place powdered sugar in small bowl. Shape dough into 1-inch balls; roll in powdered sugar, coating heavily.
10. On cookie sheets, place balls 2 inches apart.
11. Bake 13 to 18 minutes or until set.
12. Immediately remove from cookie sheets to cooling racks.

Chocolate Crinkle Nests

Cake Mix Fudge Crinkle Cookies Ingredients:

1 box devil's food cake mix
1/3 cup vegetable oil
2 eggs
1 tsp. vanilla
Powdered sugar

Cake Mix Fudge Crinkle Cookies Directions:

1. Heat oven to 350 degrees F (325 degrees F for dark or nonstick cookie sheets).
2. In large bowl, stir dry cake mix, oil, eggs and vanilla with spoon until dough forms.
3. Refrigerate dough 15 to 30 minutes, or as needed for easier handling.
4. Shape dough into 1-inch balls.
5. Roll balls in powdered sugar.
6. On ungreased cookie sheets, place balls about 2 inches apart.
7. Bake 9 to 11 minutes or until set.
8. Cool 1 minute; remove from cookie sheets to cooling rack.
9. Cool completely, about 30 minutes.
10. Store tightly covered.

Nest Ingredients:

1 cup sweetened coconut
1 bag candy-coated chocolate eggs
Green food coloring

Nest Directions:

1. In quart-sized plastic zip-top bag, combine shredded coconut and two to three drops of green food coloring.
2. Seal bag and shake to combine, adding more coloring a drop at a time until desired color of green is reached.
3. Set aside, assemble your other ingredients and preheat the oven to 350 degrees.
4. Prepare Cake Mix Fudge Crinkle Cookie dough and refrigerate 15-30 minutes, until firm.

5. Once dough has firmed up, using a tbsp., scoop and roll into 1 1/2-inch balls.
6. Coat each dough ball in powdered sugar.
7. On ungreased cookie sheets, place balls about 2 inches apart.
8. Pop in oven and bake 9 to 11 minutes or until set.
9. Cool two minutes, then, working quickly, make thumbprint indentations.
10. Fill each indentation with a sprinkling of tinted coconut, about 1 tbsp. per cookie.
11. Fill each coconut "nest" with three candy-coated chocolate eggs.
12. Carefully remove cookies from cookie sheet to cooling rack and cool completely.
13. Tip: Jelly beans or pastel malted milk balls would also make good "eggs"

Vanilla Cake Mix Crinkle Cookies

Ingredients:

1 box vanilla cake mix
2 eggs
1/3 cup vegetable oil
1/2 cup powdered icing sugar

Directions:

1. Preheat oven to 350 degrees F.
2. Line two baking sheets with parchment paper or silicone baking mats.
3. Set aside.
4. In a large bowl, beat together the cake mix, eggs and vegetable oil until smooth and completely combined, about 2 minutes.
5. Use a 1 1/2 Tbsp. cookie scoop to portion out the cookie batter, then roll into balls.
6. Place each ball of dough individually in the powdered icing sugar and toss to coat completely.
7. Place each sugar-coated dough ball at least 3" apart on the prepared cookie sheets.
8. Bake for 10 minutes until lightly golden and spread out.
9. Allow the cookies to cool for 5 minutes on the baking sheet before attempting to remove to a cooling rack or serve.

Cinnamon Vanilla Crinkle Cookies

Cookie Dough Ingredients:

1 cup all-purpose flour
1 cup powdered sugar
3/4 tsp. baking powder
1/2 cup butter softened
1/2 tsp. vanilla extract
3/4 tsp. cinnamon powder
1/4 tsp. salt

Cinnamon Sugar Mix Ingredients:

1/4 cup powdered sugar or as needed
1/8 tsp. cinnamon powder

Cookie Dough Directions:

1. In a large bowl, mix together the following dry ingredients for the cookie dough – flour, cinnamon powder and salt until the ingredients are well mixed evenly.
2. In a different bowl, mix together the butter and powdered sugar (one cup) until sugar is dissolved.
3. Also add the vanilla extract and mix with the butter sugar mixture.
4. Pour the prepared butter sugar mixture to the dry flour mixture and mix well using a spoon to form a crumbly mixture.
5. Then knead with your hands to make the cinnamon cookie dough. In case the mixture is still crumbly and you have difficulty forming the dough, you may add about one tsp. of water or milk and knead again to make the cookie dough.
6. Cover the cookie dough and place the cookie dough for about 10 minutes in the refrigerator.
7. To make the cinnamon sugar mix for rolling the cookies:
8. In a bowl, mix together the 1/4 cup powdered sugar and also 1/2 tsp. cinnamon powder until they are evenly mixed.
9. Keep this mixture aside until the cookie dough is chilled and we are ready to bake the cookies.

Cinnamon Sugar Cookies Directions:

1. Preheat oven to 350 degrees F.
2. Layer a baking sheet with parchment paper.
3. Make small balls out of the prepared cookie dough (chilled dough) and roll the balls in the cinnamon sugar mix that we made.
4. Place the cookie dough balls in the baking sheet, make sure to leave some space between the cookie dough balls as they will expand while baking.
5. For best results, roll each of the cookies once more in the powdered sugar & cinnamon mix so they will have more coating which will help in creating beautiful crinkle patterns!
6. Bake the cookies in the preheated oven for about 14 to 15 minutes until they are lightly browned on the edges.
7. The cookies may look too soft at this point, but it's fine as they will harden enough as they cool down. If you bake for more time, the cookies can turn hard.
8. So once they are baked, immediately transfer the cookies from the hot oven.
9. Allow the cookies to cool down, enjoy.

Key Lime Crinkle Cookies

Ingredients:

2 & 1/2 cups all-purpose flour
1 tsp. baking powder
1 tsp. Key lime zest
1/2 tsp. salt
1/2 cup unsalted butter, softened
1 & 1/4 cups granulated sugar
2 large eggs
1 tbsp. Key lime juice
1/2 cup confectioners' sugar, sifted

Directions:

1. Whisk together the flour, baking powder, zest, and salt.
2. Set aside.
3. Using an electric mixer on medium speed, beat the butter and sugar until light and fluffy.
4. Add the eggs, one at a time, mixing well after each addition.
5. Mix in the lime juice.
6. Reduce mixer speed to low.
7. Gradually add the flour mixture, mixing just until combined.
8. Refrigerate dough for 30 minutes.
9. Preheat oven to 350 degrees F.
10. Line baking sheets with silicone liners or parchment paper.
11. Place the confectioners' sugar in a small bowl.
12. Using a tablespoonful of dough at a time, roll chilled cookie dough into balls. Then roll each in confectioners' sugar, making sure to coat thoroughly.
13. Place cookies on the prepared pans, leaving about 2 inches between the cookies.
14. Bake 15 to 18 minutes, or until the edges are lightly browned.
15. Cool the cookies on the pan for 5 minutes.
16. Then transfer them to a wire rack to cool completely.

Sweet And Salty Peanut Butter Crinkle Cookies

Ingredients:

1 & 1/2 cups all-purpose flour
1 tsp. baking powder
1/4 tsp. baking soda
1/2 tsp. salt
1/2 cup unsalted butter, softened
1/2 cup creamy peanut butter
1 cup firmly packed light brown sugar
1 large egg
1 tsp. vanilla extract
1/2 cup mini chocolate chips
1/2 cup confectioners' sugar, sifted
1/4 cup finely ground potato chips
Salt, to taste

Directions:

1. Whisk together the flour, baking powder, baking soda, and salt.
2. Set aside.
3. Using an electric mixer on medium speed, beat the butter, peanut butter, and brown sugar until light and fluffy.
4. Mix in the egg and vanilla.
5. Reduce mixer speed to low.
6. Gradually add the flour mixture, mixing just until combined or a few streaks of flour remain.
7. Stir in the chocolate chips.
8. Refrigerate the dough for an hour.
9. Preheat oven to 375 degrees F.
10. Line baking sheets with parchment paper or silicone liners.
11. Stir together the confectioners' sugar, potato chips, and salt in a shallow bowl.
12. Using a tbsp. of dough at a time (I use a #60 scoop), roll the dough into balls.
13. Roll each ball in the coating mixture, making sure to cover completely in a thick layer.

14. Place the cookies on the prepared pans, leaving about 2 inches between each cookie.
15. Bake, one pan at a time, 8 to 10 minutes, or until the cookies are lightly browned. (Refrigerate the remaining dough between batches.)
16. Cool on the pan for 5 minutes.
17. Transfer the cookies from the pan to a wire rack to cool completely.

About the Author

Laura Sommers is **The Recipe Lady!**

She lives on a small farm in Baltimore County, Maryland and has a passion for food. She has taken cooking classes in Memphis, New Orleans and Washington DC. She has been a taste tester for a large spice company in Baltimore and written food reviews for several local papers. She loves writing cookbooks with the most delicious recipes to share her knowledge and love of cooking with the world.

Follow her on Pinterest:

http://pinterest.com/therecipelady1

Visit the Recipe Lady's blog for even more great recipes.

http://the-recipe-lady.blogspot.com/

Visit her Amazon Author Page to see her latest books:

amazon.com/author/laurasommers

Follow the Recipe Lady on Facebook:

https://www.facebook.com/therecipegirl

Follow her on Twitter:

https://twitter.com/TheRecipeLady1

Other Books by Laura Sommers

German Christmas Cookbook

Christmas Hot Chocolate Recipes

Christmas Fruitcake Recipes

Christmas Cookies

Christmas Pie Cookbook

Christmas Eggnog Cookbook

Christmas Coffee Cookbook

Christmas Candy Cane Cookbook

Christmas Gingerbread Recipes

Christmas Stuffing Recipes